PENITENT>ARBITER

Joey Gould

LILY POETRY REVIEW BOOKS

Copyright © 2022 by Joey Gould
Published by Lily Poetry Review Books
223 Winter Street
Whitman, MA 02382

https://lilypoetryreview.blog/

ISBN: 978-1-957755-00-7

Cover design: Martha McCollough

For Penny & Jenn-Jenn

"For good or for bad
It's like a valentine
From your mother
It's bound to melt your heart"

> *-Jenny Lewis & The Watson Twins,*
> *"Melt your Heart"*

Contents

PENITENT>ARBITER

Establishing Shot

[the camera glares up in circles

& cuts away to somebody crying,
washing up without their glasses on.

Their sink near a window
with a bird feeder

unforgivable birds

every poem's pretentious gaze
at that window

as the sink gurgles & sputters
hot tap & purple nitrile

the day after throwing dirt
on their love's plain pine

somebody is washing up
after Shiva: they say

the first bird you see is your fate

they're superstitious
as a distraction

or succor, & it's a nuthatch
on the side of the pine tree

& that's unfair
how could they be a nuthatch

when they laugh
& the nuthatch laughs too

arrogant in its tree
the story flickers in its beak]

SPLEEN

"Adieu to disappointment and spleen. What are men to rocks and mountains?" -Jane Austen, *Pride and Prejudice*

Absconding

When I left my job I folded my apron like always, tucked
into my hat. Six months after the supermarket rows—apples

stacked once twisted & picked—I check into a dive hotel
in Chelsea with a room the size of my body but free apples

at the desk. At the ferry, a storm culls the sky like a produce knife.
Rain, rain, passing front, then stars: belligerent dappling apples,

sparkling cider in dark sky over Governor's Island, Lady Liberty
bright as a promise. Squint long enough & any tree will bear apples

or maybe they're given us to sample on arrival at the farm
in the sparsely-paved orchard with unheard-of varietal apples,

varieties that re-live summer when sliced, cry & bleed sugar—
cold mustering a nor'easter backstage for after apple

season, the pond cool enough to sting skin while dragging
the dock from its posts to the boathouse. Andy takes an apple

but leaves a basket of late peaches. Uncle!
I had lost my admiration for you. I'm sorry, dear apple,

for leaving you in fascist rows, for the poorly-cut quarters,
for the bruised side hidden under a PLU sticker. Apple:

I remember being a mouth full child. Let's get there sweet,
because we're all going somewhere to be apple-

sauce. To the loud world, its musty-colored figs, the long
whalebone skeleton people marry under, dead apple

orchards when out of season. Gaunt capillary networks
dull white as a Macoun inside, bone-core of an apple

thrown out the car window on I-95, radio blasting Lady Lamb
on a cyser-crisp Sunday, singing: *you are the apple.*

I'll carry my past in a tucked-away apron pocket. We all do, we all
secret away what we found: a kiss, a glimpse, an apple.

I'll never leave the store. Or my heart won't, that bloated, red
goat. How I run from it. How I should hold it soft like an apple.

Essential Coworker, August, 2020

for Jenn

ASMR   pumping the manual jack—
move with that weight on a string &
we unload the pallet

past each other's turned back   laughing
listen to us haunted by a wounded movie character
listen to the watermelon   if it's ripe

I would let you see the first slice   its crystalized
sugar the aux cord   that Pisces   bowing us in a kitchen

& its garlic bread warm & did you require
a ripe case? A case cutter? Did you want
all my feelings about September   birdwatching

the day after Frank died?   From our home
store a slab of lamb & scotch   our shared hearts
digress   we're working the same 6 AM shift

right now   listen   the machete cuts a melon
& another color   cuts a shiva or a 1st birthday
some food   months starved so an angel

or a sho☒et   it doesn't matter the knife
I thought I'd see your arms full of bread
during my eventual   merciful death

here in the rabe & the edible aloe
from whence we came to a barstool
ashes to oranges to a screwdriver

& a battery glowing in the night
making it home before the storm
with a week's worth of food

7

Revelry

for Shari

I promised you a happy poem but
I've worried about what Moshe said

near Ben Yehuda street,
soldiers breaking up a fight
& me all feverish—

I promised you a happy poem.
Eldad held a cool rag
to my body until it broke.

>>>

I promised you a happy poem.
We're in Cambridge,
your baby showing as you dance.
They call our names.

I want you to remember me
in yellow tights

the candlelit backroom
where I left my book.

Three (of) Swords

the magic is not in the deck
but you, choosing to face your gnarly
cliff with its murderous wind   o dear
this was going to be about Wuthering Heights
but I can't, the mirrors all glare terribly.

>>>

It's not you glaring but what has been
done to you. Nightmares,
you can't move as the bus arrives.
There's a blood glyph, a spear
of rosemary. It's going to be cold.
The cat can't retract her claws
or hop onto the bed

o child let's talk

talk like you believe you'll mend
though you might nae, though
you should drink less

o Prince

of Cups it's all you have without
bars to troll. Your place of power
gone takeaway, the wounds naked
on your chest—three whole swords
plunged

o time

the witnesses were chastened
by what they'd seen, earnest tears.
Haven't we enough harm?

>>>

It'll be tardy when the curse
is translated. What I can promise
is hindsight sauntering
into class late with a coffee cup.
Cool kid, the one who'll save us all—

you field of violets,
you desperate apprentice.

Fruition

I slept with Anne Sexton
last night
next to me
45 Mercy Street

open at the spine
to "the divorce papers"
a song left behind without
post-production,

unfinished it fills me
with purpose
& a glass of scotch
to dull

the sound of sawing,
I am a carpenter
making two degree
cross-cuts into pine

if it takes all my allotted time.
I am a swallow
insistent blue machine
swooping insects

making figure eights
in the air, I am ready
for forever—to eat
everything I collect,

yes I want
the mistakes:
to have another drink
at two in the morning

to stay the night—
even knowing
the flatness of my image
in the long shadows
of the morning
before the sun
really gets up.
Broken like that

tentative lightness,
that unfinished
posthumous section,
I am a faucet

with no cold tap—not
tepid, I was never
finally edited,
I will never be.

3 Spleens

I respect the kidneys, I love the liver, but fuck the spleen.
Blood who's confused when to clot.

O schistocytes. Chemo suite.
O slow flow of plasmapheresis.

I drew a lover a spleen one summer,
on the cover of a card, waiting for her train,

the car's windshield functioning
as a ten-year-old's magnifying glass. Later,

the concert, too loud behind her house, went late—
somebody's spleen, I suppose.

Why can't guts keep calm?
The liver filters, the eyes behold! The spleen

does sudden things to the blood. I could

carry her to the other side of a good cry—
then the red blood cells ripped,

caught on a thrombus. There was nothing for it,
for our inconsolable spleen: it botched

the clotting factors. The surgeon excising
the love between us shrugged,

the nurses put away the paddles.

o dear widow

for Jaime

praise to you   flying that flag
with its skull posed in wilting
fronds   the sparrow heaping seeds
next to mate felled by a pane
of glass   separation from
the home you were promised
as a child   instead a shard
of that house   a slice of a slice
your demesne   the small floorplan
living   an occluded sort-of-sky
making the stairs   barely making
the stairs meet   bare stars
gleam on your sons' cups

praise to the tattoo before it fades
dark marked   banded black into a pot
of soil   holding a pen   how do you keep
an appointment?   how do you open
your eyes or log in or make it
to the next branch?   winter juncos
early   draping cold   drawing
the days closed   a few hours for lovers'
snowballs but the hand from your hand
rigid   what is the opposite of a star?

praise then that black sun   that spikes
in your sons' child-hand drawings
you felt a sharp circumference

so praise your geometric spleen
with sines   portents   one spoon
clinks the dish   one hand in the snow
hoary harbor   nee an exfoliated
arborway a mile down the road
[murmurs a memory of oaks]

praise memory   that manicured park
where the trees absolutely lit for
picnic eves   wine slosh   the faeries
hadn't fled   smiling deaths upon
your family of eyes   all your many
fumbling arms   you will remember
the will-o-the-wisps

so praise to haven   any footsteps
across your hardwood floor
you used to go to sleep smelling like the beach

praise to the poppy-red wind
warm announcing a storm

praise to his wake   [as waves]
the drop in temperature after [his wake
like a boat's]   writing his story
on yourself   you become god
isn't that comforting   sleep

praise relaxing of hands   there he's
written into your skin a date   the sixth
day you lifted the water ban   now rest

praise the 12 shards that shape
skin-skidding you-scraped rocks   listening
to the sea breathing   empty skein   love
one long abrasion

praise to a cove conceiving its own
salt   in dark pink the old story water
carved o painted o burnt where love lives
archaeologically   taking the whole sea
in its mouth   spit out fountains foams
waves   the stories they tell stain the glass

praise you still with seeds chirping
as the winter birds seep   as they
turn you into carbon   you trace
elements around your memory   as the stars
twinkle their thousand soliloquies   they say he sleeps

Lacuna

I knew Lucifer, impelling me but kind
about my winged shoulders
& I ran over cobblestones
at midnight, past witch
shops & ghost museums.
Dreamy long-hair days, hexes
precise there like Hecate,
Thessaly. Assonance, meter
of the name in my breathing
after the bordello folk slipped
out the side door, hotel bar, last
call & the bitch in me wishes men
misfortune this night
but not him, looking toward
his hotel & the harbor behind
in the decision time between
late & early. When exactly
will I get to bed, & whose?
& whose hoodoo? His catching
me with my leggings down
after the John, hot scotch
breath—the Puritanical hotel
now Romantic, the lacquer-wood
railings of stairs led to a small
room &   us   whose fault
in the night?

ABJECT

"I was afraid to be alone / now I'm scared that's how I like to be"
-Azure Ray, "November"

ABJECTION

I want to hear what you hear
in a cheap recording of yourself

without markup, distortion,
or chorus. I want to say

>>>

At the glory hole, metal punti,
scalding orange spear
of an arrogant hunter

but a spell's a spell & she left
lights on while undressing—

Imagine us in the Salem woods
furnace-bright at the dusk window:
glass soaking in annealing flame,

blinds open to boggy April nights.

>>>

Sharp stick, then
the gather had us molten.

Helpless cat loves a light purr
& kneading, curl-ball, ear-twitch
swagger. That's until the ceaseless

napping. Helpless sleep. Both of us
looked good in that argyle frit—
& made that out of glass.

>>>

I had waited a year
& unexpectedly, another week

so I ran to the gas station,
disappeared into the oven,

those night hours to cure
months of longing—

Sinai

after "Obedear", by Purity Ring[1]

I was born days after the sea split
like a dropped melon,
like an unbarred chest.

In two years we'll reach the first
olive tree. Ghastly sand,
Where has the rest gone? Predicaments

of dark water, decades confused by
the ruse of circumference—god
send radii, god send rain that stays,

in feet of soil. I never touched
calf's gold below the sleepy mountain
where our leader disappeared.

Guilty, we never see Autumn done up
like henna, like drifting to sleep.
O dear when the sky's low—

how to keep the sabbath?
Fall is brief, dangerous storms, shattered
pots in cool caves. Subterranean

lovering, keep to nights. Impossible
stars, shuffled & oily, smear the sky.
When we reach Kineret they'll finally

[1]Purity Ring. "Obedear", *Shrines,* 4AD, 2012

crispen. So soothes my hunger, yet
who can say bereftness won't follow
to the next shrine   to the water line

down a long yellow hall, ungold,
ill amber. Don't just wander back
& forth. Arrive at the grateful seas

of dreamtide: a beach ready
for our penitence & sleep.

Siren

But that's years ago, no magic
remains for us/ the siren instead
shouts the back door of her shady-ass
dad's flat in Attleboro from the road

& it's not a hex bag/ something
for aloneness/ the volume knob
has an unexpected fractal effect/
the opposite of a prism/ shushing

as a sign of real danger/ she heard
sirens but she never asked what
I heard/ the knocking
& further back in the room

the opposite of a fan/ emergency
on the side of a box/ a container
of used sharps at her hospital

job/ the opposite of therapy/
But she sung elegant wrecks/
she does it to survive/

Jenny Lewis Was in This Place, and I, I Didn't Notice

A rust belt guitar chord as survival tactic,
Americana some bullshit about losing
car keys & minor fires. o love
Jacob's Ladder wasn't a story
about getting up in the morning—
how simpler they had it, never crying
in the backroom of a Stop & Shop,
nor at the cusp of a lit-up bridge, never
over an acoustic rainbow-colored
sunset, thinking it were better
they weren't born or no one had
learned the formula for almond milk.
Where are you, Gabriel? I need
at least a few rungs. I need to wrestle,
spit & rename myself, then live
in exile for twenty harvest cycles,
drawing water, working fields
of some unpronounceable staple grain
& I can't speak it, but it's gold
& delicious with lamb. When I get home
my blind father will cry, too, realizing
it's all been a country song,
a mistake, a rising action. We'll sup
& remember our blessings. We'll spread
the damnedest mint jam, tho.
We'll pet the dogs who run, run smiling
to anyone who comes in the door.

Pithom & Raamses

You say these names like I should know them,
in my hearts of hearts, a deep forge,
a weakness for brick. Exposed brick in my first
apartment, I am above this. I work a double
shift & earn a notice to quit. In those days
you could run away across a sea—they had it
easy. Whose pyramid are you building, do you
even know? So you can't even run.

ABJECTION

Think of the place you go to hide
from your own bullshit. Where
you remove your hide. They call it
a hide, I called them daddy, baby,
useless patronizing. Have you
seen the marsh in April, clean
of the summer algae? It'd be easier
if I could go to a time, but god
gave us places [& worse, lovers].
One called me *Marsh Heart*
but we weren't looking in front of us:
purple dead nettle & henbit.
The boy swaggering & his ax,
another with a filet knife.
One's impish tendency to edge
& left on read as a fetish.
I intend to show them all
then they misspeak, lecture me
the woods a mile from home
& only I can see the boy,
& only I can see the ax.
I prefer to walk alone, then
meet them darker, sipping rotgut.
He said *you have a thick*
hide when I bent, bent. I wanted
to take him here. I wanted
to walk drunk into nettle
& get scratched but it wasn't
April, it's never anymore.
That's my place of power,
dammed & milled. Loops

& an old orchard. Mid-spring.
Sun in Aries. Boy, I can hide
from me inside you or hide
my cruelty in bottoming.
We know who's not calling,
who has acres for days.

ABJECTION

(1) damp

Like an octopus thrown on the Garden ice
& you were expecting shattered glass
loud calamity   but it's a dull limp

forget the movie montage's map-scanning
& dungeon scene. Sleep,

sleep in soft comas instead of noise.
Bethany hates sleeping alone
but I've always liked it. I've begun

craving it, getting balled only
like a cat on sofa-back. It's not
what you were expecting, loves.

I'm sorry for icing it. Entropy
octopus, both disappointed &
gross to handle barehanded.

Like instead of a white knight
you got someone chain-smoking
outside a bar.

>>>

(2) melanoma

But that's my oblivion, what's yours?
Maybe it's the DJ
wearing a full face shield

a song too slow to dance
so you shoegaze
like you learned in the small clubs
of Central Square.
One night the band sound-checked
an hour before letting us in
& were jerks about it.
I made myself think about that
instead of the small risk growing
in your skin. You're post-op
in the middle of an epidemic,
slower than anything
that could hope to save you.

>>>

(3) tarot

he scoffed I said the magic
isn't in the cards—it's in prostrating.
Honesty. Lower the lights

because in any case the truth holds
pleasure & keening:

when I was 13 years old
draped in god & singing to him
holy, holy, holy

this is what I was praying to & it came
in the mailroom but first in a canoe

of all places. This is what I was praying to,
illicit & ruinous!

>>>

(4) veracity

This is the truth I arranged
with fanned strawberry
for a garnish. The truth is
a necromancy of octopus
but it's also amuse-bouche.

Truth is a knee-slapper, brigand & rake.

Time was we went to the tavern
with the whole town.

Truth was there eventually.
Problem was the SOB didn't show
until civilians had died.

9 of Swords

I love lying so I wrote a book called "I Will Not Stab My Own Self
with All These Knives". I denied whispering the desiccation hex
& then said I'm Fine when the wasting came. It was my wasting.
Look here at my perfect set of porcelain wounds: a little ribcage
sticking out, a bit of blood, a general chipping around the eyes.
Tell me I'm a poor, sick child. Pick me up.

CANDENT

"Stars at my eyes
stars at my feet"
—Cocteau Twins, "Shallow Then Halo"

Aubade with Stir-fry

for Kolleen

The others in the living room,
knifework & coins cut
with turmeric. That's the secret
garden, brick courtyard
with mourning dove. My heart
an unfinished manuscript
until this slapdash
spice blend. Cumin wins,
that's the secret.

empathy

       when
first you imbibe his words
you really take them in. all.
they are water & diffuse into you.
you feel it in your bones
like arthritis or

are you mainlining ice?

inside you
the river empties into
a lake at a newly
connected delta

eddies of sadness & mirth
befuddle your boat
toward a submerged stone;

>>>

       when
he thrust his hands into
the snow you
also felt submerged
in cold

listen:

<<<

       before when
he told you *She's gone*
you selfishly slipped into
his body to eat
his grief.

you hadn't tasted
the truth
the pillars of salt
since the November
of fallen
& left

the first time you ran
your hand over the earth
& father's half-submerged stone.

>>>

            now
you can't watch him wash the teapot
across the kitchen

so you walk over
the fire-glaze

tile
you laid down together
& slip your arms
around his & hold them into
the warmth

pull the submerged
ceramic up out of the suds

clean. suddenly
this is &
this is hard
indivisible labor.

Junco

standing on top of the new snowcrust in my last good yard
where grosbeaks came in the spring on top of the box where we
offered seed. Tides have tides, seasons have seasons, moods have
moods & we spent some years building houses in shop class for wind
to savage them. It's paper & feathers, all of it. They appear as soon
as the sky calms. Only don't forget that juncos consider this south.
I trust you to do with this what you always do: build a fire in the
woodstove & put on boots.

Portmanteau

after "Stardew" by Purity Ring[2]

I know it seems far   how you moved
before the lockdown   careless like that

how you knew *starry blood & bloom*
I realized   driving in a brief snowsquall

attached to three separate shadows:
from the streetlights, the cloying

dashboard greenlit, & a voice
milky singing her ribcage come

light or shade   she hit the lights
& the room plunged   hit darknotes

of a sweet height & floatvoice
near my exit   less pavement

more snowdrift & hearing
highway lines, edges that snap

back to an absent singing distance
seems far   but just be where you are

safe as houses   safe as sins
thick as dew on the first violets

love I promise the violets are purpling
the raw March yard   I always loved you

[2]Purity Ring, "Stardew." *Womb,* AD, 2020

& here you are, with a basket of groceries
so I can hide, saying *I know it seems far*

but just be where you are   calling
me   before calling yourself   before

eating in the morning   praying
for bread or manna stardust

on the already glowing clover
we were looking for four-leaf

we were throwing a ball in the yard
I was listening to you sing

gone live from a sick city
& someone offered

someone offered a mask

CANDENT

after "Amenamy" by Purity Ring[3]

K— asked me where I was from as I drove him down the Lynnway
drawbridge toward the airport

 & sun poured across the beach, candented sun that burns your eye-
lids green when you close them

but we didn't stop & he had a flight back to his shattered fawn, the
middle of America,

lakes he knew, accents that made sense, mostly the impedious o of
wind curling

rusting factories & cities that eagerly die, withdraw, those sad lovers

behind him in a bright photo & I was speeding to make a party later
but dark hair

shielded his gardener's eyes with the windows free from their gaskets,
glint-metal plumb

swinging on my rearview mirror tethered between us & the Earth's
core

catching then losing then catching the demi-sun of a hazy May noon.
Breathe out the windows,

anyway I'm from here—where my grandparents met on this beach,
then held for 72 years.

[3]Purity Ring, "Amenamy." *Shrines,* 4AD, 2012

CANDENT

At the southwest edge of Broadmoor, a small pond filled by a beaver dam

straddled route 16. The dam had flooded ten feet of trail but rocks gave enough dry
   footholds to cross.

A weasel rattled the riverine marsh reeds & skittered up, sniffing my boot, uninterested

& then back into the dense field. Water trickled toward the park, under the boardwalk

to the wildlife pond, then the Charles & I was windswept over H— who never made it

this far with me but to the other acres of wildflowers & swallows in all the nesting boxes,

& a family of less ornery swans than I'd ever known. In five years the dam disintegrated

the water moved east, slowly rising until it broke paths & renegotiated where we were
   allowed,

the sign said *trail closed,* then even that submerged. But it was there,

we kissed there like idiots in the temporary—

The Oracle

Poindexter on a Friday afternoon knocking on the boss's office: hey

there was a manufacturing defect in the heart. I'd like you to pity me

my body. I always had abject panic to fall back on. Replace wisteria-wound rail

with iron portcullis—that's when I feel alive. When I notch another survival

in God's old yearbook, sign in the corner but harsh words. I love

you I do now please lambaste my little figurine. You almost caught me

saying wee fetish. You almost thought I cared.

CANDENT

I sneak past the dugout, behind the bleachers, & over the outfield fence to smoke up.

The mechanic neighbors giving me side eye through the screen door call the cops

but it's night so the police cruiser searchlights the baseball field half-heartedly.

I throw my kit in a bush & break for the treeline like a spotted deer into the trails

behind the school. There's Hale-Bopp in the canopy gap, my only directional until
    an open field:

in this terror peepers, tall grass, a stream running loops.

in this terror a comet & early fall's ecstatic sweetbreeze,

settling into a tentative high under the just-noticed eyelets, sky-holes poked for my
    fleeing body

Cartographist

We'll bathe often in light of the moon
We'll sew clothes from **the stem of** our **womb**
We'll bathe often in **light** of the moon
We'll sew clothes from the stem of our womb

Oh, my **sweet** fairy
The past is strong, strong, strong
Touch not my bosom for I'll not get far, far
Color your **cartography** in your **dreams** of me
Maps will not lie, will not lie, will not lie in me

Grow into gardens, the caverns you found in me
Heal off the weightless you held from the start of me

Oh, **my sweet** fairy
Our hearts did us wrong
But **rudders** of bodies doth carry us on, on
And more moons than our eyes can recount and store

Yet they **bid** that we see the same things
Sweet, they **bid** that we swim in their sea

Well then, **the amber woods** are pouting
Lie down to keep our heads from falling
Give in to **these seeds** beneath me
Measure that they do in time harvest

—

"Cartographist"[4]

the stem of womb-light
sweet cartography dream—
heal, my sweet.
Rudders bid the same,
bid the amber woods
lie down these seeds.

[4]Purity Ring, "Cartographist." *Shrines,* 4AD, 2012

ABJECTION

after "Bodyache" by Purity Ring[5]

When I moon I'm hearing her—
I'm dark as sleep, last as a lost oar
in the brackish, boiling mixture

swirl-humors, scars of the never-
healing bodyache. How to survive
hearing her abject vocal timbre?

Everyone since fits on the other side
of Libra. I tried to falsify the records,
masked, with a flashlight. Catsnatcher,

body burglar, sleeping for weeks, split
by a man in his third-floor disaster
pad. I know how to shamble

away, but not her same unreeling:
thrown from a speeding bicycle
in Colorado winter. Dimmer switches

spool light & I'm limping
from a cold boy's apartment.
Since I shot my own foot

like a man I want her to know
how hard I'm hurting. I want
to know what's her quietest feeling,

[5]Purity Ring, "Bodyache." *Another Eternity*, 4AD, 2015

48

as if I could keep my vicarious
hands. Lie awake? I swear
I let her sleep like that,

caught her leg under a table
in meet-cute glee. Afterbit, tho,
I can't fix my teeth.

I did what my body ached,
I slept in hell. That was my name,
could I write anything sadder than my name?

ABJECTION

after "Stillness in Woe" by Purity Ring[6]

In the back shed   place of dust vials
someone holds an axe
to his chest   enough to draw
blood   less gentle than she'd hoped
but breaking the skin impels clarity
so you're welcome. Imagine a dusk
pervasive, world-ending
no-wind still, where she's unmade
from the spools & belay loops
of the society of men. Unrigged
haunted ship!   they say, used to
being dull in remove. Not this alone.
Meet her in a snowglobe moment
worthy of her keep—build pillow forts
but metal, but dangerous & weighted.
He's right to be afraid of her whetting.
Blue bed kingdom, cloudy sea glass
disorient him. He waits the storm out
in a wind-harangued tent, island-bound
under an anvil sea-fed thunderhead.
Dare he cross the sparse-grassed field
to the toolshed? *Run to her now.*

[3]Purity Ring, "Stillness in Woe." *Another Eternity,* 4AD, 2015

Raincalling

I used to call a new lover *a gust of wind*.
I don't call that more
than anyone calls. I wouldn't call
anyone rain but there's one
reliving embers of a pallet-fire
that was last. Taurus around the sun,

rain matting pollen to the ground, unlike sun.
We needed rain, we needed callback wind
more than a gust of nothing, fire
a night bedroom. Allocate more
rain here, a handsome one.
I'm too tired to call

for takeout. *I'll-pay-if-you-call*
kind of romance. Sporadic sun
on the island but claim one
deduction, an acrimonious wind
making the chill more—
that's its due. No further fires

at sport. Swords to ploughshares, fires
left holstered for a call
at approximate time. What, more?
What word from heaven, sun?
That God sometimes broke wind,
we're looking for just one

reason to believe. One
rip in the mountain air, one fire
man hadn't captured & winded.
A lark, I call it. Call it
revenge of the heathen sun,
enchanter, cellist & more.

Of the throngs of many more
I found this one
& back they go. They sun
their hides by a small fire
& a tent. When natures call
one wins, the other winds up

with less. More limbs for the fire
serving one. call your call,
rain the sun, rain your wind.

A Wicked Wind

after "Stranger Than Earth" by Purity Ring[7]

I'm in my car blazing Purity Ring because *We are stranger than Earth with the seasons misled/ Stronger than the moons*

& when we pulled each other out of it tonight after celestial disasters like walking out of the building into the rabbit night as the persnickety automatic lights dropped us into dark

rooms full of chairs & we bump into them so when I run into the desert & someone's coming over the soggy, purple bluff

we're projectile, honestly, but kind behind our experiment tables

seeking science to buttress us *When our parts parted*

she bled and bled and bled I was in a dress in the theatre looking out to the punch-drunk limelight holding up an elegiac friend, a different dearness than the acts in the couched lounge in twos

& when we cried into the audience, then into someone else's room *again, again, I wasn't thinkin' 'bout you/ I wasn't*

& it's sung because we know it's a lie, when we're the self-aware, the yearning yawn or object of propaganda, but breathe: we can watch the cars go past. *There is no lesson in magic—*

was it ever comforting? & against the trick of Aries we thought it was. *Pity seek what we might lose But in a week might our weakness elude.* & those weeks were ours

they were ours

[7]Purity Ring, "Stranger than Earth." *Another Eternity,* 4AD, 2015

YOU SAY

"Slow down so I can catch you, slow down" – Múm, "Slow Down"

If Someone Doesn't Know You Should Tell Them—

—about the moon's moon & the scientist cat, the huntress who left mouseguts on

a new patterned rug still taped to the linoleum. Or how in America the guts is us.

Tell them you voted today in the small room named after a mill owner whose name

is stamped all over town. Tell them men with a backhoe have come for his mill.

Our ways of telling have changed, so tell them with the one white rose to freeze

it in a block of ice. No, tell them to come over. Tell them to try their thumb or

at least where, let them know where the spot is on your back. Tell them they feel

sturdy & look tall backlit by the bathroom light. Tell them they are an absence

when you see them from far away. The simple question they asked reminds you of

when a baby grabbed your hair, softly, nursing a water-warmed bottle. If they want

to understand how you taste they need to study the moon's sign. Tell them the test

will be a cumulus. Give them a fair chance to answer. The hardest part is the silent

blinking of the cursor after, the three moons pulling inches every year, waves

receding without their pull.

Maths (MISSING DATA)

a half-eaten breakroom cake
"good   uck   job"
in the frosting benediction
from a supermarket
& do you feel guilty now for
the time you dropped
an orange   or 500 oranges
& to the punchclock at the first minute
you could   we were so young
& thought we could   we were raised
in these fields of desiccated corn
we were born with these:
weaponry   the wrong
classroom assignment
the board was filled with them
differentials & integrals
we're integrals & we used to walk
down Newbury street talking about
sucking cock during the conference
making it home half the time
how dare we   what math
would figure & how far did that love
move   three time zones
& when I said I was coming
I lied   but I washed dishes
at your apartment
in the outskirts of LA
behind the sign
when I die I'll say
I saw a hill once & we walked close
to your husband
short-sleeve shirts
& somebody's car & all of us
in a parking lot drinking beer
in the middle of the city's bell curve

GEZELLIG

She taught the kvetch of an owl: blissed out canals of Amsterdam holding hands, black-feathered. Whose loud synesthetic concert hall full of overripe Mogwais. When she busted his chops he'd say, Who cooks for you? Mostly she cooked. Who couldn't get whose mouth around the vowels, bus-drivers mocking. Who walked across the field of onion & leek, waiting for a duvet, hoping for the moment to string topaz along her wrist, but it rained that day & the next. Whose travelog with a bird claw mark next to Nijmegen where they shared a book in bed. The bed was *gezellig*. Her grip enthralling enough to survive the bathroom breaks love begets. An airline strike, a ladder to a second floor of a Dutch castle where the tour wasn't in English just yet. When who wanted to learn the language, Henny said, *It's not a language, it's a throat infection.* To wit: *het is goed*, she made quesadillas with what was called 'Old Cheese'. Monkeys & eels cheered, the sun out until 10 at night, swinging outside the farm. Who must admit how those years felt: *gezellig*.

Another Day in Paradise

The damn light flickering in the breezeway
again, all the nephews in dinosaur costumes
knocking at front doors in unison
when all uncles just put the action movies in.
Stagger back to the couch & next thing you know
the alarm is doing whatever annoying thing
you ask, no, beg of it each—call it dawnish,
reach for the comfort of a travel mug.
God, it's just coffee, Jane. Stopped at that light
that takes for-ev-er, after two hours you watch
 a church girl take a violin from a case, wishing you were
that terrific a kid, or holy enough, something.
She sees you watching her, I'll bet she'd
play if you pled for gospel. At work the apples
are bent, we're out of left-handed pickles & crystallized
ginger. The pallet lopsided, deli kicking the kombucha
off. Everyone asks for the lefty pickles. Suffer it for a buck,
for a nephew-hug & the cool drip of a Dino Egg
brand plumcot in that corner of the backroom
the camera can't catch. The pallet jack catches
every case, stacked & stacked & stacked in a cross-hatch
for weight stability. The customers come past
& everything is theirs if they want it, if they'll
take it home with them to their veloci-nephews,
who peel them, roaring, bite in, it's a bloodbath,
the pulp everywhere. Uncle, down the hall,
screws in a new bulb. *There,* he says, *perfect.*

Poem for Adrianna

A dead sparrow in a front yard absent of grass—
its brightness slakes the neighborhood seal point

& Ade *hopes it had a good life.* Kiddo, I elide the cat's
murderous blue eyes. I stop telling her how

I've had to survive—generations pinced
themselves with rusty tools. The song sparrow's call

for a ringtone. Off, off the phone. Did M— tell
the boy I still hate him? Is he still next to a lilac?

Never mind, I shouted at the lilac. The sparrows prefer
little cracks above the neighbor's windowsills.

I want to sleep in her bedroom nearest the nest.
We buried flowering seed with the half-eaten bird,

then visited our shameless new kittens.
I'm holding one in my hand, barely

mewling, & I wonder how many birds she'll hunt.
Those same blue eyes. The cat was me

before I really loved. That comes late in our kind.

Maths (The Taylor Series)

It started as the chaos of an equation

& how to describe the integral space
holding under unreal functions

with Greek & graphed pictures
like square lithograph prints
of the curve, of the sculpting math—

chaos unmeasured for centuries until
Taylor theorized beautiful polynomials
approaching exact facets of maelstroms.
One may define an ugly function,
a few minutes of calculated risk:

risk to find powers, consider zero, seek
the wind-blown coefficients to a stillness,
charter symmetry between narrow isles,
order   prime   & solve, build
evidence to an understanding
that the beautiful & ugly facets of any X
would approximate the same
integral space.

A12 After a Concert

Full after a meal,
we recline,
this night different
from a normal night
in the way the cool hits
our overwarm bodies.

Sated, ears popping,
hardly hearing Bjork
on the tapedeck singing
"All is Full of Love"
on the A12

& the radio leaves a wake of sound waves
skipping over the pond.

Streetlights morph & distort
Nicky's half-sleep half-smile,
Karen's knuckles curl
& cuddle the steering wheel.
We listen listlessly
every hard breath of soft
night air we sigh.

My forehead touches the glass,
and melts into condensation,
I am parched, but drink
2 am like I've been desert-crawling
in this oasis of chilled glass.

In the dark,
eighth notes scatter behind us.

Boy?Girl Goes to the Movies

Boy I am a girl I am a sojourner here
in a land of gendered bathrooms
as far as the eye—

>>>

I craved certainty, plausibility. I
could pass & that came with dope
concierge service but boring clothes.

My mother bought cream eggs &
she asked me, *do you feel*
like a girl? I didn't know how to answer
but drew her into an overlong hug.

>>>

The moment when Grant says AMPHIBIAN DNA

>>>

I know I avoided
more of the locker-slamming & circling
bikes   the teachers who deliberately
deadname   but the boys weren't kind
behind the Mellon Street barn
& I wouldn't have had the words
even if I wanted to tell them
I didn't know how to ride
I didn't know how to braid
I wasn't any of what we knew
but I pled down to perjury
& my hat cut in half by mean boys

\>\>\>

my hair buzzed on one side
down to my other shoulder
in a purple turtleneck
before one of the Scream movies
taken by S— then I told her
if I was a girl I would want to—
& she was already trailing away.

\>\>\>

this was after G—'s 2Q2BSTR8
makeovers & the queers are
sometimes not alright. There was
a power outage midwinter
when we lit candles & played
No Truth Just Dare. All that
made me feel dumb about feelings

\>\>\>

~~I needed to be just a *little* repressed~~
like hey tongue-kissing
before a bunch of people get stabbed
admittedly sounds bad out of context
but I LOVE Junior Mints
& being forced to shut up
because otherwise I can't remember to.

Trailer Trash

"Is it not somewhat reluctantly graceful, to be/ thrown away?" —July Westhale

You're fucking in someone's living room,
setting down a picnic basket, sharpening a spear
or it's a knitting needle in the most comfortable blanket fort
or it's your high heels stabbing at the boys' ear drums,
spoiling for a fight

like they stand a chance, like the sign hasn't always flashed lavishly
in all your neon letters. The moon's first word was your name
& then it couldn't spin. The rain's destination is a porch with your boots,
because just enough mud, is that a blood stain? Nail polish,
you lie. When you say things they're not such a stretch.

I like how you say *spigot* as if it's not ridiculous,
all the sounds people make. You love them in their own way,
tea or beers. Across the country in a trailer, bumper sticker:
I lost my virginity but I still have the box it came in.
You're driving with some schlub who was supposed to be shotgun

DJ. That was a lie, but the kind of thing you'd do—
letting the miscreant sleep, allowing them the aux cord
when they had to sound, touching an imaginary mustache
for dramatic effect. In a truck-stop town you find karaoke,
sing for them. They sing back. See? Watching someone sleep

is a responsibility. You're crisscross on the bed
you've bought for a night. In stories most things are metaphors
if you listen to their faint hum, what quasars sound like: distant stars.
At the end of everything, having confirmed your theories,
you ride a horse over the sun because the horizon seems pedestrian.

Feel it in Your Bones

I'm an arrowhead-chipped skeleton
dug up by some old love
& his roses upon roses   except
I've never been brought flowers
guys   guys just buy Camels
he's throwing cartons
at my dessicated face   charming
thinking of the old concrete college
sandbox   I'm seriously over 30
& the U has hoisted three new dorms
upon the fae hillside like sparrows
I can feel it in my neck before each
adjunct quits like a haruspex
like the Kindly Ones   I'm so beyond
linear uses for scissors now   where's
the next snip   maybe if I felt that
tensioning before the twinge I could've
taken the keys from

>>>

a student of mine tonight
was about to break a valve
how useless this empathy
all our magic against the incoming
student woe   or roses or smokes

I'm glad to be past the age when any of this
fucking surprises me   god I hear
clanging against my ancestral tomb

Black Milk

Rainbows in a puddle reflect the triangle over Kenmore.
I took a shower with a boy, we poured
parabens through the threads. In some places
the tap water catches. The town with a fire
underneath—most hair has that underglimmer.
Most chalk advertises in two colors on a black skin.
Our rotating taplist serves slicks & sheens,
then we boycott breast milk, or. Or pipes
that will outlive the tribes on the plains. Those shitwits
use horses, our fracked stomachs are heartier.
Some of us still lie supine at night, but I?
Someday in that pine forest as roots. Until pipes.
In case of pipes, no roots. The topography of here
rows of udder structures on a flat stomach
of rock. But how shiny the hair! Directions:
drink this dark rainbow your parents gave,
their parents gave, laced with Paracetamol. Laced
with something to help you sleep.

[Charoset with Bitter Herb]

The women trudged, dough on their bodies & the Sinai scorching enough to bake unproved cakes

a good example of how wishing hurts.

Our Lady of the Aspiration, water-lunged or oven-backed. Of avulsions & blister like matzah crust.

Our Lady of the Chazzan & No Congregants for the call & response, so they call-call-call, & there's only one doll so the kids become jealous

of their names for it & their fan-fic. In the time before the time before the corruption of the word my doll was first in the new belly of universe—

did we mention the bread? How Passover is my favourite metaphor for our blisterness.

How far can a promise be from here? lol:

don't follow your compass, but learn how it works. Eat off the ground if you must. Save how you can. Your safety requires blood. First-born may die.

---

brisket so tender I ate it with my soup spoon

Tsimis, the stew with apricot & prune, sweet

poured out wine for

thousand thousand thousand thousand thousand

dead dead dead

---

when I was six I continuously screamed yaheil midbar which means *the sands of the wilderness* in Aramaic or Hebrew, the Song of David, my middle name

was hyper & I locked my muscles & screamed the sands of the wilderness

not realizing how dark my mouth was & how quickly flash floods could make bones
of a passenger van

& my parents were used to this from me so they put up with it until Friday
when we arrived at shul. After l'cha dodi came the Song

of David & the sands of the wilderness
so then we knew why but it didn't stop me from screaming

---

you feel a kind of succor in writing your name
on everything—
you've run hard to that one safety, the dream of crossing
sea on dry land,
such a lullaby for adulting. That slavery will be punished,
men will die
if they don't look like you. You're eager to slay the ram
from your own
herd in the name of the Angel shohet, blessed be.
Paint its blood
on your doorposts if you wish to live.

ANNEALING

*"There I go / There I am / A life of gold / How long I've been driving
Fall into happiness / Wish you could be here"*
                                    —Phantogram, "Into Happiness"

Spring Thaw

I'm over a cold—
tentatively— & the snow
backflips into rain,
streams make the side streets
of Somerville clean
o I never believed
that rain were sweet
but sweet! Breathing
through both nostrils
again, & what's left
of the clumps of snowbank
doesn't affect parallel parking.
The small mound of brackish
white on Summer Street
melting. There, I said it
in a poem about snow
but I meant a head cold
or I meant winter cheeks
slapped hard by wind
& I meant my car
& my knees are melting
America is melting
Greenland is but
sometimes a human
walks up a hill & down
the other side of the city
pausing over their last cough drop
considering how geography
suddenly makes them see
the whole city in sweet.

CANDENT

This is the last time this year I'll stand in the rain as the weather breaks

gladly, feeling the surge & ebb as rain pours then mists then pours

& I'm weightless, I'm part of the storm, I'm falling from the gutterless roof

& this soaked brown dress flaring from where my body forgot to curve

towards the Blackstone river, night-dark & ready to swell, I mean the water

ending up roaring. I sent the text myself so the rapids are mine,

placing rocks here, and here, when the still was low. I have seen this river

dead as a desert & up to the road. We watched cars swerve from a national park.

High & judgy, sitting on a rock with my left leg underneath me—one hike

& we knighted ourselves, naked as a lucid dream feels, wandering train cars

wishing there were more than ripped seats & track clacking. The lie lay bare

as floodriver cracked bridges west of the dam. Tributaries cheer

the river, fed by a human back. Ink birds. It goes on without us for miles.

CANDENT

Andrew pulls a coat on, the door's undraped window bright with him. We're for a late dinner & colloquy evening, clear of cloudiness, brittle as crackling snow when I dig a foot into its bank— I'm not exactly cold but brisk ale, drawn out like a teenage night. How fatuous is contentedness? Still, three new posts hold & we rest our drills for Christmas. I will sprawl my bed like the cats lie, still. Claws languid for sleep. Those darlings! Gratitude pours out of my eye holes. No, that's not it, one needs to lean into tonight. The droid finds memories in an old friendship, the first friendship. No, no one dies. The throne melts into a pile of gelt. Today a deck melts off asbestos, drill-bit countersink routing us flush. The building inspector runs his hand, points, then signs. Each of us nods, spits in the dirt with equal gravitas. Now I'm watching Andrew, ready to build his first home. The frosts were hard, but sublet to hard sun. Maybe, maybe I can—

the bones

for July

Next to a ribcage she read
from the book of dead birds.
Maybe it was a whale jaw
& she read from a museum.
She's a museum of tarot,
a bookshelf of good advice.
No-one else stood a chance
next to those slate bones.
She could break bones, in case
of emergency break the glass
to summon her from tea,
from staring at a blade of grass.
Obliged like promising to keep
Sabbath: thankfulness. Obliged
like waving pedestrians to safely go.
Oblige all the first-period students
to write an ode, teaching
Joseph's dream to them stars,
all tapping anxious implements
on the laminate. When I forget
how to poem she whispers: *ulna,
femur, tarsal. Whip up some
sinews, gurl.* She's on a plane
clacking keys, she's exhuming
rare tulip bulbs. Her greenhouse
like a snapshot of Flevoland,
windmills spinning, rows & rows
of flowers for bones. The glasses
of water by the bay windows
in the small houses
clean, but the bone chimes
toll in the distance.

Acknowledgements

I'm so grateful to Eileen Cleary, Martha McCollough, Christine Jones & Lily Poetry Review for the hard work & loving attention they have given to my work.

Of many friends & poetry acquaintances whom I thank one & all, standouts include July Westhale, Shari Caplan, Kolleen Hoepfner, Andrew Gould, Diddle Knabb, Khaya "Khalypso" Osborne, Joey Phoenix, Hannah Larrabee, Kazim Ali, Sara Siegel, Robbie Gamble, Jeanne Obbard, Sara Afshar, Erica Charis-Molling, Stephanie Angelini, Hannah Wagner, Heather Hughes, Hawthorne Lindsay Smith, Erasmus More, Sam Witt, & JD Scrimgeour.

Thanks to Poetry Society of New York, especially Stephanie Berger, Nicholas Adamski, Jackie Braje, Gregg Emery Vance, Charlie Layton, Jane Freeborn, Emi Bergquist, & Kendalle Getty.

Tip of the hat to Purity Ring for writing such engaging songs.

In "Boy/Girl" I refer to the Steven Spielberg classic, *Jurassic Park* (Amblin, 1993).

"Trailer Trash" borrows its title & epigraph from July Westhale's poem of the same title.

My tarot deck, gifted to me by Diddle Knabb, is Slutist Tarot. Khaya "Khalypso" Osborne set tarot poetry prompts that guided me in writing.

Previous homes of poems from this collection:

Bad Pony, "Candent [This is the last time]"

District Lit, "3 Spleens"

Drunk Monkeys, "Black Milk"

Five:2:One, "empathy" & "Spring Thaw"

Hard Work of Hope, "Essential Coworker, August 2020"

Lily Poetry Review, "Another Day in Paradise"

Live Nude Poems, "A12 After a Concert"

Miniskirt Magazine, "the bones"

Molecule, "Pithom & Raamses"

Moonchild, "Abjection [When I moon...]" & "Portmanteau"

PSNY's Poetry Brothel Anthology, "Trailer Trash"

Roi Fainéant Press, "9 of Swords", "Abjection [In the back shed]", "Boy?Girl Goes to the Movies", "Establishing Shot", & "The Oracle"

Sudden Denouement, "Absconding"

Some of these poems were workshopped or shared with Salem Writers, Boom Zoom Hour, & virtual Poetry Platform.

& thank you, too.

ABOUT THE AUTHOR

Jessica Lynne Furtado // jj lynne photography

Joey Gould is a writing tutor from a town originally established as a utopian society. Since 2011, they helped orchestrate each iteration the Massachusetts Poetry Festival in Salem, MA. In addition, they have written articles for Masspoetry.org & traverse MA as a workshop leader for Student Day of Poetry events in schools. They volunteer for The New York City Poetry Festival & perform as Izzie Hexxam in The Poetry Society of New York's Poetry Brothel. Always willing to entertain, they have joined a poetry circus, improv comedy/poetry events, & a poems-to-order art gallery event. They curated a special issue section of *Soundings East* as a returning fellowship alum of & generative workshop leader for The Salem State University Summer Poetry Seminar. A poetry editor in their own right (formerly of *Golden Walkman* & presently at *Drunk Monkeys*) their poetry can be found in issues of *Five:2:One*, *Lily Poetry Review*, *District Lit*, *Memoir Mixtapes*, & *The Compassion Anthology*, amongst others. They have been a Mass Audubon member since 2008.